AMERICA'S MOST WINNIN

ALABAMA FOOTBALL

BRIDGET HEOS

rosen publishing's
rosen central®

New York

Published in 2014 by The Rosen Publishing Group, Inc.
29 East 21st Street, New York, NY 10010

Library of Congress Cataloging-in-Publication Data

Heos, Bridget.
Alabama football/by Bridget Heos.
    p. cm.—(America's most winning teams)
Includes bibliographical references and index.
ISBN 978-1-4488-9402-4 (library binding)—ISBN 978-1-4488-9424-6 (pbk.)—
ISBN 978-1-4488-9425-3 (6-pack)
1. University of Alabama—Football—Juvenile literature. 2. Alabama Crimson Tide (Football team)—Juvenile literature. 3. Alabama Crimson Tide (Football team)—History. I. Heos, Bridget. II. Title.
GV958.U513 H46 2014
796.33263—d23

Manufactured in the United States of America

CPSIA Compliance Information: Batch #S13YA: For further information, contact Rosen Publishing, New York, New York, at 1-800-237-9932.

CONTENTS

INTRODUCTION

Quarterback A. J. McCarron sat on the bench in the stadium known as Death Valley, weeping. The Louisiana State University Tigers had had the University of Alabama Crimson Tide on the ropes throughout the second half of the November 3, 2012, game. The Tide had been down 17–14. Though it was only November, a chance to play in the BCS National Championship game was on the line. Alabama was undefeated, but so were three other teams. Maintaining, or rather fighting for, a perfect record was essential.

And that's just what Alabama had done. On Alabama's 28-yard line with just ninety-four seconds remaining, McCarron completed four out of five passes, culminating in a screen to running back T. J. Yeldon. Yeldon navigated a minefield of LSU defenders for 28 yards to score a touchdown. After scoring the field goal, Alabama was up 21–17. LSU had time for a last-ditch effort, but it did not pan out. Alabama had won. So why was McCarron crying?

"Just so many emotions running through me," he explained in a November 4, 2012, SI.com article. "Sometimes it can be a lot of pressure playing here at this university, especially with all the tradition of winning and everything."

Alabama Crimson Tide quarterback A. J. McCarron and running back T. J. Yeldon celebrate a game-winning touchdown against Louisiana State University, November 3, 2012.

Alabama has indeed won its share of football games. And to this day, the Crimson Tide is considered the team to beat. When sports writers discuss who will make it to the BCS National Championship game (the bowl game that determines the national champion), they often add "besides Alabama." It is almost a given that Alabama, as the number one–ranked team in the nation, will make it to the big show. But the game against LSU proved that in football, nothing is a given. Every victory must be hard-fought. Outcomes can be unpredictable. (That was made all the more clear the following week, when Alabama was upset by Texas A&M.) That is why the game is played.

To learn about the tradition that Alabama players must rise to each week—both in practice and in games—read on. You will learn about everything from the program's humble beginnings to its legendary coaches to its toughest players. You will learn how the Tide rolls.

CHAPTER 1

THE TIDE RISES

The University of Alabama, home to the Crimson Tide, is located in Tuscaloosa in central Alabama. With approximately thirty-one thousand students, it is an NCAA (National Collegiate Athletic Association) Division I school. The football mascot, an elephant named Big Al, is symbolic of the historically big, strong, and fast line, and the team name, the Crimson Tide, refers to their performance on a field of red mud in 1907. The Crimson Tide has won fourteen national championships, including in the 2009 and 2011 seasons, led by coach Nick Saban. Their most famous coach is Paul "Bear" Bryant, who led the team to six national championships during his twenty-five-year tenure.

Of course every team has to start somewhere, and that's usually at the bottom. In 1892, six decades after the school was founded, W. G. Little, a student, started the football team, named the Cadets because Alabama was a military school at the time. Nationwide, football was an emerging college sport. It had begun on the East Coast and then spread west and south.

Little was the team captain, and the coach was E. B. Beaumont. Alabama's first game was played on November 11, 1892, against Birmingham High School,

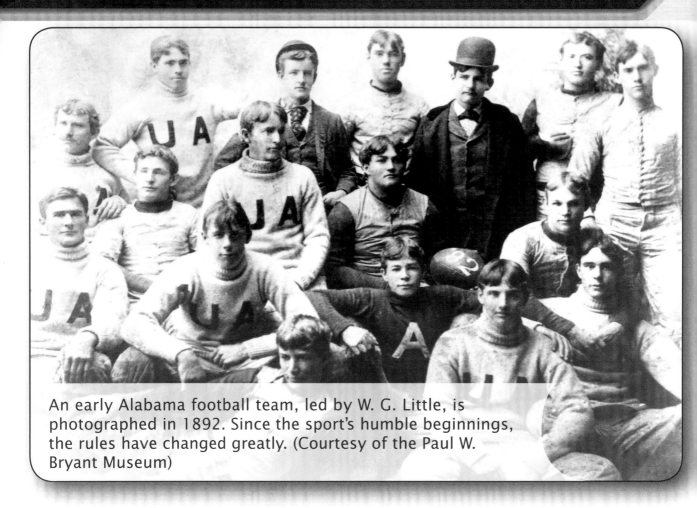

An early Alabama football team, led by W. G. Little, is photographed in 1892. Since the sport's humble beginnings, the rules have changed greatly. (Courtesy of the Paul W. Bryant Museum)

a team of players from several area high schools. Not surprisingly, the college team won 56–0, but the following day, they lost to the older players of the Birmingham Athletic Club. The Cadets won in a rematch but lost to Auburn in February, going 2-2 in that short first season.

Coach Beaumont didn't return the next year, and in 1893, Alabama won no games. The team became known as the Crimson Whites, for the school colors. Football was an emerging sport, and the rules were in flux. At the time, it was a lot like present-day rugby. School leaders thought the sport was too rough, and in 1898, there was no team. Actually, the sport was controversial nationwide, and for good reason. Several players had died from injuries incurred while playing. In 1905, President Theodore Roosevelt threatened to ban the sport if the players weren't better protected. That year, officials from top college football teams formed safer rules for college football. The group evolved into the NCAA.

At Alabama, school leaders relaxed their grip on the football program and eventually became advocates of the team. The team got its present name in 1907. Alabama was playing Auburn, which was strongly favored to win. But in a muddy brawl, Alabama tied Auburn. Because the mud was reddish and the Alabama team rolled down-field like the tide, a Birmingham sports reporter called Alabama the Crimson Tide. The rival teams would not meet again until 1948.

In 1912, Alabama football got a staunch supporter in school president George Denny. Denny Field opened in 1915. That year, Alabama, led by tackle W. T. Van de Graaff, won an important game against Sewanee, a small private school today, but at the time a football powerhouse. Alabama hadn't beaten them since 1894.

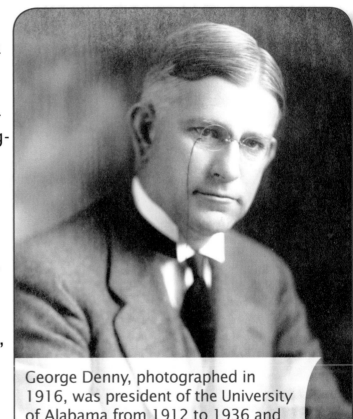

George Denny, photographed in 1916, was president of the University of Alabama from 1912 to 1936 and a staunch supporter of Crimson Tide football. He is one of the namesakes of Bryant-Denny Stadium.

Denny knew the importance of a strong coaching staff. In 1919, he hired horse-racing reporter Xen Scott, who had played college football. The East Coast, as the birthplace of college football, then had stronger football programs than the South. On November 4, 1922, the Crimson Tide traveled outside the South for the first time to battle the Pennsylvania University Quakers. Alabama had taken the lead but then lost it. With a fumble in the end zone by Pooley Hubert, all appeared to be lost. But Shorty Propst recovered the ball and scored. A strong Crimson Tide defense prevented the Quakers from scoring in a Hail Mary attempt in the final quarter. Alabama won 9–2. Scott's team was greeted at the Tuscaloosa train station by thousands of cheering fans. They had

ALABAMA'S TOP THREE RIVALS

Auburn Tigers: In Alabama, where there are no major pro sports teams, college football is king, and nearly everybody cheers for either Auburn or Alabama. The two teams met in Alabama's first season, and to this day, an Alabama season is considered unsuccessful unless the Crimson Tide beat the Tigers in the Iron Bowl.

Tennessee Volunteers: Alabama first played Tennessee in 1901, then not again until 1928. The Volunteers won that year, establishing themselves beside Alabama as a great southern team. The teams meet on the third Saturday of every October.

Louisiana State University Tigers: Coach Nick Saban created a football powerhouse at LSU, then left to do the same at Alabama. They're now two of the top teams in the nation—and they reside in the same division. This rivalry may not have the history of Alabama-Auburn or Alabama-Tennessee, but nationwide, it's considered one of the best games to watch.

proven that the South was a force to contend with. The tide was turning.

ROLL TIDE!

Scott had established a tradition of coaching excellence. But throughout the season, he had been in poor health. He retired, and the team hired a new leader: Wallace Wade. Wade wasn't exactly a teddy bear. His players feared him. They weren't allowed to date girls under his regime, and if they ran into him while holding a girl's hand, they would drop her hand. Wade's hard-nosed approach worked, however. His record was 61-3. And an undefeated season in 1925 earned Alabama a trip to the Rose Bowl. The oldest of the bowls, the Rose Bowl at the time determined the national champion. In spite of its record, Alabama was the underdog to the University of Washington Huskies. There was a stigma that southern football teams could not compete against eastern and western teams. Wade led the Crimson Tide to a tight victory, 20–19, against the Huskies in a game some football historians call the most important game in southern football history. During Wade's tenure, a new stadium was built in 1929. It is now known as Bryant-Denny Stadium, named for Denny and Coach Bear Bryant (a later name addition). Wade would win two more national titles before being succeeded by Frank Thomas.

Thomas was able to read his players and motivate them. A former Notre Dame quarterback under Knute Rockne, Thomas ran the Notre Dame Box, an offense known for its shifting backfield and trickery. It had worked for Notre Dame and now worked for the Crimson Tide. The team won two national championships during Thomas's tenure. Thomas also established a tradition of recruiting. He offered

Fans fill the Bryant-Denny Stadium for a spring game on April 18, 2009. Seating capacity is 101,821, and every home game since 1988 has been sold out.

a free coaching clinic to high school coaches. This gave him the opportunity to meet coaches who may have talented recruits. It also improved high school football, thus improving the field of recruits.

Of course, no offense runs itself. Quarterback Millard "Dixie" Howell and future NFL hall of famer Don Hutson led the team on the field. Hutson was a multiple-threat player. As a runner, he was elusive; as a receiver, he was tough and unpredictable. At the 1935 Rose Bowl against Stanford, Hutson caught nine passes for 160 yards, ran for 111 yards, and punted six times for a total of 262.8 yards. He also played baseball and ran track, sometimes all on the same day. Hutson went on to play for the Green Bay Packers as an end, safety, and kicker (often kicking his own extra point).

The opposite end to Hutson was none other than Paul "Bear" Bryant. Bryant was the eleventh of twelve children in a poor family. He grew up working on the family farm in Arkansas. Standing 6 foot 1 (185 centimeters) and weighing 180 pounds (82 kilograms) at age thirteen, Bryant was a natural fit for football. He played on the Arkansas state championship football team but finished his high school requirements at Tuscaloosa High School after being recruited

Paul "Bear" Bryant, in his signature houndstooth hat, coaches a November 6, 1982, game against Louisiana State. He began his football career at Alabama as an end alongside future NFL Hall-of-Famer Don Hutson.

by the Crimson Tide. Like many players, a football scholarship was Bryant's ticket out of poverty. He would be the first in his family to go to college. But when Bryant's father passed away, he told his cousin he was quitting school to come home. His cousin, in an effort to rile Bryant up so that he would stay the course, wired, "Go ahead and quit, just like everybody predicted you would." That didn't sit well with Bryant, and he decided to stay. His resolve hardened to epic proportions. In 1935, he famously played an entire game against Tennessee with a broken leg. Though a solid player in his own right, he referred to himself as "the other end," knowing that Hutson's talent overshadowed him. Bryant would of course prove his football talent in other ways.

In the first ever NFL draft in 1936, Bryant was selected by the Brooklyn Dodgers (then a football team). Like many players, he turned down the offer. Professional football salaries at the time were low; players could make more coaching even at the high school level. Bryant took an assistant coaching job at Union University in Tennessee. He returned to Alabama as an assistant coach under Thomas but left for a series of assistant and head coaching jobs, as well as a tour of duty in World War II.

World War II ended in 1945. In Alabama, Frank Thomas was leading the team to another national championship at the Rose Bowl. The 34–14 victory over Southern California on New Year's Day, 1946, marked the final Rose Bowl matchup for the Crimson Tide. (Beginning in 1947, teams were chosen for the Rose Bowl from the Big Ten and Pac-8.)

The following season marked the end of an era. Frank Thomas was forced to leave his coaching post because of health problems. His record was 115-24-7. (The 7 stands for ties; until 1996, Division I football games could end in a tie.) The year 1948 marked the rebirth of a tradition: Alabama played Auburn again in an annual matchup that became known as the Iron Bowl. Alabama won 55–0.

The 1950s saw its share of superstars, with Bobby Marlow rushing for 233 yards in a 1951 game against Auburn and scoring three touchdowns. In 1952, Coach Harold "Red" Drew's record was 10-2, putting him in league with Xen Scott, Wallace Wade, and Frank Thomas, who all achieved double-digit wins. Quarterback Bart Starr had wanted to play for Bear Bryant at Kentucky, but attended Alabama to be closer to his girlfriend. He started only one season as quarterback in 1953. That year, Alabama defeated Auburn 10–7 to earn a spot at the Cotton Bowl against Rice. Alabama was down 7–6 when Rice player Dickie Moegle received a handoff and headed for the goal line. He got past every Alabama player on the field. That's when Alabama fullback Tommy Lewis came off the bench to tackle Moegle, in a head-smacking moment that went down in college sports history. He later explained to a reporter, according to the Paul Bryant Museum Timeline, "I'm just too full of 'Bama." Referees awarded the touchdown to Rice, who won 28–6. Lewis was largely forgiven by Alabama fans for his crime of passion. Starr became a star quarterback for the Green Bay Packers under legendary coach Vince Lombardi. And Alabama would soon welcome home Bear Bryant.

CHAPTER 2

MAMA CALLED

Bear Bryant developed a strong reputation by turning around the football program at Texas A&M. But he had always pined for sweet home Alabama. When he took on the head coaching position at Alabama in 1958, he explained, "Mama called. And when Mama calls, then you just have to come running" (quoted in *The Junction Boys: How 10 Days in Hell with Bear Bryant Forged a Championship Team,* by Jim Dent, and elsewhere). It was the beginning of an era. Bryant was a tough leader, and he attracted a certain type of player, namely, tough ones. Even some of the toughest players didn't make it under his regime. His grueling training sessions were legendary. (His ten-day Texas A&M training camp was described in *The Junction Boys* as pure hell.)

When practice began in August, Alabama was sweltering hot. It was a different time, and back then, players weren't always allowed water breaks. This was a dangerous practice; players often passed out from heatstroke. One player later described how he tried to hydrate by sucking the sweat off another player's jersey. In the night, players could hear other players' suitcases rolling down the hall. They were quitting.

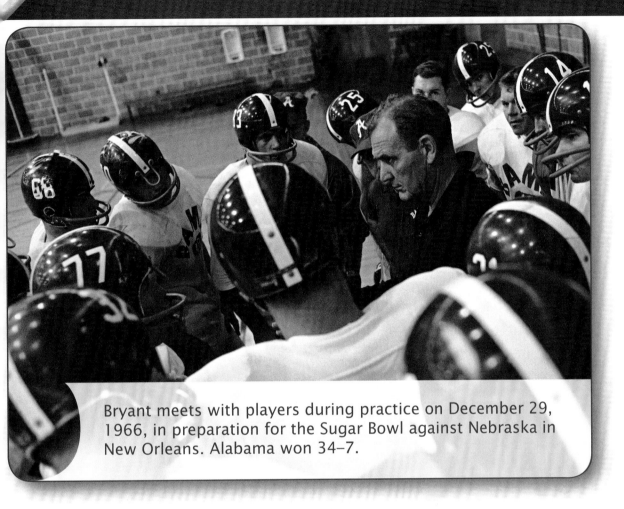

Bryant meets with players during practice on December 29, 1966, in preparation for the Sugar Bowl against Nebraska in New Orleans. Alabama won 34–7.

But for many of Bryant's players, a college scholarship meant they would be the first in their family to finish college and have a brighter future. Either they weighed the long-term benefits, or their parents forced them to stay on the team. They also took pride in surviving college football's toughest program. If they made it to the NFL, they were respected by other players who knew what it meant to play for Bear Bryant.

Beyond his toughness, Bryant cared about his players' big-picture goals. For instance, John Croyle told Bryant he wanted to open a ranch for abused and neglected children. Croyle wondered if he should pursue a career in the NFL first. Bryant advised Croyle not to join the NFL unless he was committed to that goal. Bryant supported Croyle's dream of helping abused children by donating to the ranch, along with Croyle's teammates and local business leaders.

The early 1960s brought Orange Bowl wins and national champion titles. Legendary quarterback Joe Namath led the team to many victories, even with an injured knee. Bryant called Namath "the greatest athlete I ever coached," according to *Bleacher Report* on July 31, 2009. Lee Roy Jordan dominated on defense, making 31 tackles in the 1963 Orange Bowl.

For all its points of pride, Alabama football had a big problem. Throughout its history, it had been all white. In 1970, it was among the last segregated football programs. Bryant wanted to change that.

THE GAME THAT CHANGED EVERYTHING

The University of Southern California integrated college football in the 1920s. By 1939, integrated football teams were commonplace outside of the South. The University of California, Los Angeles, had a backfield made up entirely of African American players, including Jackie Robinson, who would go on to integrate Major League Baseball. But the South lagged behind. Maryland football integrated with the recruitment of Darrell Hill in 1963. Other southern schools followed suit. But not Alabama or the other teams in the SEC (South East Conference).

Beyond football, Alabama was a battleground for the civil rights movement. Montgomery, Alabama, was the site of the year-long bus boycott spurred by Rosa Parks's refusal to give up her seat. Dr. Martin Luther King Jr. led that protest and went on to lead the civil rights movement. However,

Jackie Robinson, shown here practicing football at the University of California on September 20, 1939, would later be a Negro Leagues and Major League Baseball star.

Alabama also had powerful segregationist leaders. George Wallace was elected governor in 1962 with the promise, "Segregation now, segregation tomorrow, segregation forever." He personally barred black students from entering the University of Alabama in 1963, in spite of the 1954 *Brown v. Board of Education* decision that required schools to integrate. The students were ultimately able to enroll, but only because President John F. Kennedy federalized Alabama's

HOW BEAR BRYANT GOT HIS NICKNAME

Paul Bryant was a big-boned boy, 6 foot 1 (185 cm) and 180 pounds (82 kg) by age thirteen. He reportedly earned his nickname as a teenager when the circus came to town. There was a contest, in which anyone who agreed to wrestle a bear would be paid a dollar a minute. Penniless, Bryant thought this sounded like a pretty good idea. But while in the ring, the bear's muzzle came off. The teenager leapt from the ring, and as it turned out was never paid. But he did earn the nickname Bear.

National Guard, which had been helping maintain segregation in the state.

Throughout the 1960s, the football team remained segregated. Five black students tried out for the team in 1967 but did not make the team. Bryant said that he wanted to recruit black players but did not have the support of the Alabama administration or fans. He was tired of watching some of the brightest prospects slip away. He couldn't even recruit high school standouts from Alabama. His team was losing its competitive edge. Some schools even refused to play a segregated team like Alabama. Bryant needed to prove to the people of Alabama that it was time to integrate. So he scheduled a game against USC, which had many black players. Bryant knew that USC was a football powerhouse, and that Alabama would likely lose against them.

The game divided the town of Tuscaloosa, with black communities cheering on the USC bus as it rolled through town. They felt a closer tie to a visiting team that gave black players a chance than to a hometown team that would not let them play. USC had many standout players, but the superstar of the game was Sam Cunningham, who rushed for 135 yards with twelve carries, and scored two touchdowns in the first quarter. He was running circles around Alabama's defense. The final score was 42–21. After the game, Bryant reportedly told USC coach John McKay, "I can't thank you enough for what you did for me today," according to a February 9, 2012, *L.A. Sentinel* article.

Wilbur Jackson was the first African American to receive a football scholarship to Alabama. John Mitchell, a defensive end, was the first African American to play in a game for the Crimson Tide. After his college playing career, Mitchell became the first African American assistant coach for Alabama and the youngest. He went on to be an assistant coach for the Pittsburgh Steelers.

Soon after, African American Alabama player Ozzie Newsome became an all-American receiver. He said that Bryant was open-minded to talent, whether you were a newcomer or a star. But you had to give your full effort all the time. Bryant recruited many hard-working players in the 1970s, including Tuscaloosa native Sylvester Croom. Croom, the son of a preacher, was reportedly one of Bryant's favorite players. Bryant recruited Croom as a tight end and linebacker but later had him play as tackle. So impressed was Bryant by Croom's hard work that he asked him to become an assistant coach after graduation. Later, Croom became a standout head coach at Mississippi State.

Other great players of the era included tackle and guard John Allen, considered one of the top SEC players of all time, running back Johnny Musso, whose performance against Auburn in 1971 earned him a photo on the cover of *Sports*

Running back Johnny Musso rushes in a November 28, 1970, game against Auburn. Alabama lost in a close game. Musso was featured on the cover of *Sports Illustrated* the following year.

Illustrated; and all-American Dwight Stephenson, called by Bear Bryant "the best player I ever coached," according to the *Huntsville Times* on June 19. (Whether that's different than being the best athlete, or it was simply hard for Bryant to choose from so many great players, is unknown.)

A year after its thumping by USC, Alabama met the California powerhouse again. This time, both teams were undefeated. Alabama introduced a secret wishbone offense and beat the Trojans 17–10. It was Bryant's two-hundredth win. Bryant retired in 1983. He died just a few weeks later from a heart attack. During the funeral procession, fans lined the streets from Tuscaloosa to Birmingham to pay their respects to the legend. His legacy lives on both in Alabama fans and in the players who carry with them everywhere the toughness honed on the Alabama football field.

CHAPTER 3

THE TIDE ROLLS ON

Life at the University of Alabama went on, but it was difficult to fill Bear Bryant's shoes on the football field. Ray Perkins, a former player of Bear Bryant's, took over as head coach. In his second season, the team had a losing record for the first time in twenty-eight years. But thereafter, he led the team to victorious seasons. One game he coached against Auburn ended in what is known as the kick heard 'round the state. Van Tiffin kicked a 52-yard field goal, leading Alabama to a last-minute victory against the longtime rival.

Perkins recruited football legend Derrick Thomas. He had never seen him play. Nowadays, high school players e-mail highlight videos to coaches and post them on YouTube and recruiting Web sites. But in the 1980s, coaches scouted talent in person. Perkins scouted local recruits but relied on his assistant coaches to scout players around the country. Perkins first saw Thomas play during an Alabama practice and was impressed right away. In his last two years, Thomas was coached by Bill Curry. Thomas still holds many records at Alabama, including 27 quarterback sacks in a single year and 52 in his college career. Thomas was drafted by the Kansas City Chiefs, after Curry told then head coach Marty

Schottenheimer, "You will put him on the field the first day and he will be your best player, and he will be the best player that you have on the Kansas City Chiefs every day," according to an August 8, 2009, AL.com article. Thomas's career was cut short when he died in a car accident. He is remembered as one of the top Kansas City players of all time and for his literacy work off the field.

Curry led the team to three winning seasons, but losses to Auburn were devastating to his career. The Crimson Tide had a successful run under coach Gene Stallings, a survivor of Bryant's Texas A&M training camp. They were unde-

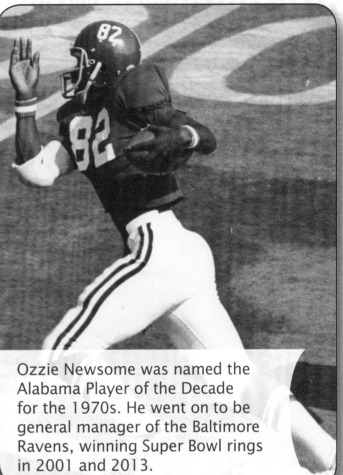

Ozzie Newsome was named the Alabama Player of the Decade for the 1970s. He went on to be general manager of the Baltimore Ravens, winning Super Bowl rings in 2001 and 2013.

feated in 1992 and beat Miami at the Sugar Bowl. However, the following year, the team had to forfeit all of its regular season games, changing its official record from 9-3-1 to 1-12. (Prior to the forfeits, three games ended in a tie; the following year, the NCAA instituted overtime play to break ties.) The sanctions were due to star Alabama player Antonio Langham having signed with an agent, making him ineligible to play. Coach Stallings believed Langham was taken advantage of by an unscrupulous agent. Overall, Stallings had a successful record at Alabama.

THE STADIUM

In the early days of Alabama football, the team played on the quad, a grassy area on campus where students can hang out. Twenty-two years later, the team got its first stadium, University Field. It was renamed Denny Field for George Denny, the university president who was also an advocate for the football program. A new stadium, called George Hutchison Denny Stadium, was built in 1929. At the time, it had a seating capacity of 18,000. It has been expanded through the years to hold 101,821. The name was changed to Bryant-Denny Stadium in 1975, to honor the longtime and long-winning coach. Every home game since 1988 has been sold out.

When Stallings retired, a rocky patch followed for the University of Alabama. Under Coach Mike DuBose, the Tide had two out of four losing seasons. He was let go in 2000. Dennis Franchione became head coach. In 2001, the NCAA released a bombshell report alleging past Alabama recruiting violations (by Stallings and DuBose). The school had to reduce scholarships and ban certain boosters from the program, and it could not play in a bowl game for two years. Coach Mike Price was fired in 2003 before coaching a single game because of a personal scandal. Next, Mike Shula had an inconsistent record and was terminated.

That's not to say there weren't great players and great victories during this time. Brodie Croyle, whose father, John, played under Bear Bryant, was a standout quarterback known for his unflappable demeanor. (John Croyle was the player who dreamed of opening a ranch for abused children; he did

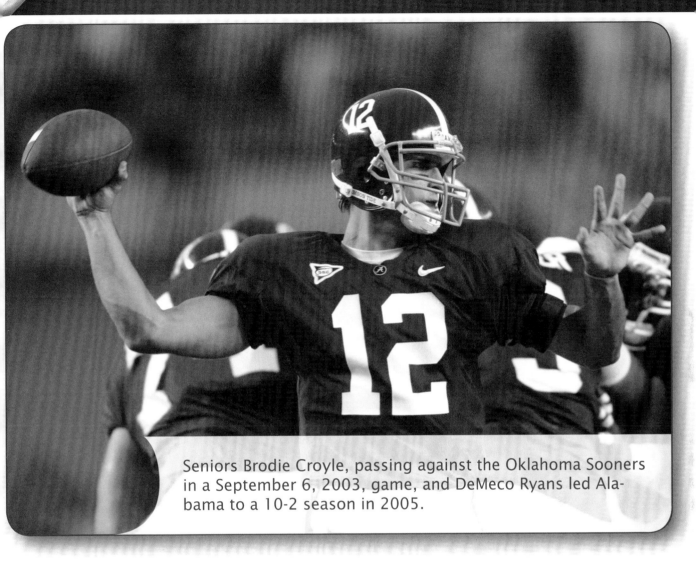

Seniors Brodie Croyle, passing against the Oklahoma Sooners in a September 6, 2003, game, and DeMeco Ryans led Alabama to a 10-2 season in 2005.

that, and Brodie grew up on that ranch.) DeMeco Ryans was a high achiever both on and off the field, earning the NCAA's Top VIII award for his athletic and academic achievements. He went on to be an NFL Pro Bowler. These two seniors, as team captains, led the Crimson Tide to a 10-2 season in 2005 and a victory at the Cotton Bowl.

But Alabama needed a leader to bring consistency back to the program. That leader was on his way. In the meantime, we turn to an entity all its own: Alabama fandom.

ALABAMA LEGACY AND FANS

In the South, loyalty to college football teams runs deep. Ninety percent of Alabamans are college football fans, and 86 percent root for Auburn or Alabama, according to *Rammer Jammer Yellow Hammer,* by Warren St. John. The University of Alabama is a large school, with more than thirty thousand students enrolled. Fifty-eight percent are from Alabama, and they probably grew up cheering for the football team. Though it is the fifth largest town in Alabama, Tuscaloosa becomes the largest on game day. Alumni and other fans flock to the school, and the campus fills with 130,000 fans tailgating on the quad. Many fans follow the team on the road, too.

No game is bigger statewide than the Iron Bowl, in which Alabama plays Auburn. Alabama's "Roll Tide" cheer is answered by Auburn with "War Eagle," a cheer that according to legend comes from a fan long ago bringing his pet eagle to a game. The eagle began flying around the stadium, just as Auburn made a victory march toward the end zone. Fans began cheering, "War Eagle!" Alabama has won forty-one of the seventy-five matchups, including the vast majority with Bear Bryant as coach. Though a historical underdog to Alabama, Auburn has had its share of winning streaks. Auburn freshman Bo Jackson ushered in a decade of change during the 1982 matchup with a game-winning touchdown known as "Bo over the top." And Alabama's rough patch in the early 2000s was made all the rougher by losses to Auburn.

The results of the 2010s' Iron Bowls remain to be seen. Auburn quarterback and Heisman Trophy winner Cam Newton led his team to victory in the Iron Bowl (and the national championship) in 2010. But Alabama won the following year. The rivalry has a fun side, but also a dark side. Coach Bill Curry,

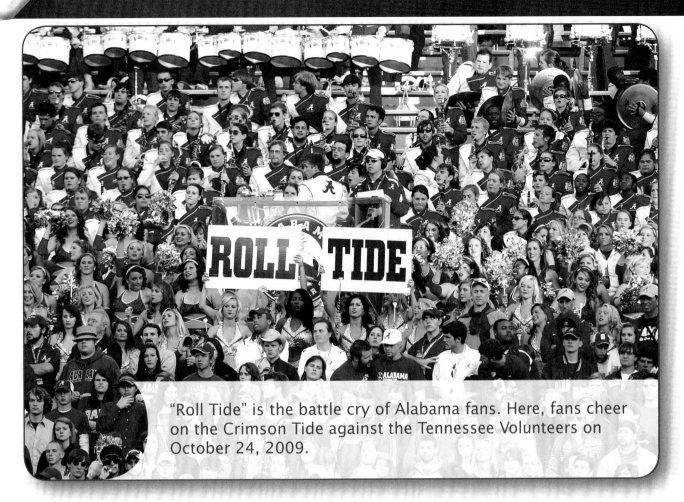

"Roll Tide" is the battle cry of Alabama fans. Here, fans cheer on the Crimson Tide against the Tennessee Volunteers on October 24, 2009.

interviewed for ESPN's film *Roll Tide/War Eagle*, said that his players received death threats after losing in the Iron Bowl in the 1980s. After the 2010 loss, an Alabama fan called Paul Finebaum's radio show to say that, after seeing an Auburn jersey irreverently placed on the Bear Bryant statue during the Iron Bowl, he traveled to Auburn and poisoned two historic oak trees on the campus. In the same documentary, the man denied the action but was brought up on several charges, including felony criminal mischief. He faced ten years in prison if convicted. Of course, that is not typical of most fans. Any time you have strong feelings among people, there are those who go to the extreme. At the same time, the more typical level of fan passion is a draw for players. Players who grew up in the South learned that football was important to people, and they want to continue to play in a place where football is important.

The Iron Bowl may be one of the biggest games of the year, but every game is a big deal. Game day traditions include Big Al and the four-hundred-member Million Dollar Band—one of the best in the nation. "Roll Tide" is perhaps the most famous cheer. But at the end of the game, fans are also known to cheer, "Hey [name of team Alabama is playing], Rammer Jammer Yellow Hammer We Just Beat the (Heck) out of You. Rammer Jammer Yellow Hammer Give 'em (Heck) Alabama." Rammer Jammer was the name of a university newspaper in the early 1900s, and the yellow-hammer is the state bird. Alabamans have put their own spin on Crimson Tide songs. Carter Hamric cowrote and recorded "Roll Tide Roll," played on the radio during football season. And Saban's Web site features the song "4th Quarter," by Tuscaloosa rap band 63 Boyz.

The SEC, currently considered the most competitive football conference, enjoys national media coverage. At least one contender each year for the BCS National Football Championship tends to come from the SEC. This attracts players nationwide, particularly from the highly competitive southern high schools, to SEC universities. Loyalty plays a role in recruiting. Sons of players return to play for the Crimson Tide, and players go on to coach at Alabama.

Fans are loyal to the Crimson Tide, but they are also demanding. They expect the best from their coaches, and they expect it in a short amount of time. Those high expectations would be more than met by coach Nick Saban.

CHAPTER 4

THE TIDE RISES HIGH AGAIN

ick Saban played football at Kent State in Ohio. He began coaching in 1983 as an assistant at Michigan State. From there, he held many coaching jobs in both the NFL and NCAA. Saban became a household name when he turned around the football program at Louisiana State University beginning in 1999. Earlier that decade, the team had endured seven losing seasons. Under Saban's leadership, the team won two SEC championships. Over the next five seasons, Saban became the third winningest coach in Division I football. In 2005, Saban was recruited to take over the beleaguered Miami Dolphins. He improved the team's record over the next two years but said there was more work to do. So fans were surprised by his seemingly sudden decision to leave the NFL to coach at the University of Alabama. While some Miami fans were critical of the move, Alabamans welcomed Saban with open arms. A crowd greeted him at the Tuscaloosa airport, chanting, "Roll Tide." Saban was given an eight-year guarantee and became the highest-paid coach in college football.

The team went 7-6 in 2007, Saban's first year of coaching. The following year, they were undefeated in

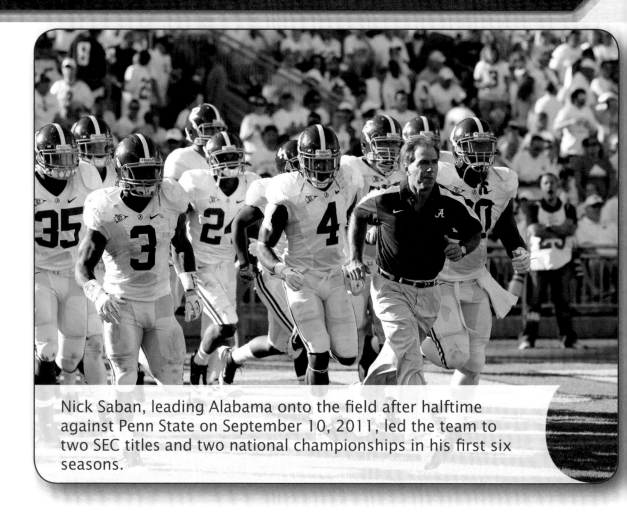

Nick Saban, leading Alabama onto the field after halftime against Penn State on September 10, 2011, led the team to two SEC titles and two national championships in his first six seasons.

the regular season. The Crimson Tide was ranked number one for the first time in sixteen years, but lost to Florida in the final minutes of the SEC championship. The team earned a place in the Sugar Bowl, and Saban was named AP and ESPN coach of the year. The best was yet to come.

The year 2009 also brought an undefeated regular season. Nonetheless, Alabama was ranked second behind Florida in the SEC. The teams collided in the SEC championship game on December 5. Florida, led by quarterback Tim Tebow, was favored to win, just as they had the previous year. Alabama took an early lead; at halftime the score was 19–13. After an unsuccessful first down attempt by Florida, Alabama running

ALABAMA FOOTBALL BY THE NUMBERS

National Titles: 15
National Championship Seasons: 1925, 1926, 1930, 1934, 1941, 1961, 1965, 1966, 1973, 1978, 1979, 1992, 2009, 2011, and 2012.
SEC Championships: 23
Iron Bowl Wins: 41, Auburn, 34 (1893–2011, with a 41-year hiatus.)
Players Currently in the NFL: 39
Heisman Trophy Winners: 1
College Football Hall of Famers: 20
Capacity of Bryant-Denny Stadium: 101,821

back Mark Ingram ran the ball three times in a row, followed by a 28-yard pass by quarterback Greg McElroy. After a penalty on Florida, Colin Peek caught a pass for a 17-yard touchdown. The Crimson Tide would shut out the Gators for the rest of the game. Ingram scored three touchdowns in all, rushing for 113 yards. Throwing 239 yards, McElroy was named MVP. According to sports reporter Pat Forde on ESPN.com, "Greg McElroy out-Tebowed Tim Tebow."

Alabama earned a place in the Rose Bowl and became national champions. Ingram became Alabama's first Heisman Trophy winner. He was a first-round draft pick for the New Orleans Saints. The following year, McElroy was named National Football Foundation Scholar-Athlete and was a Rhodes Scholar nominee. He was drafted by the New York Jets.

The 2011 Crimson Tide team, also national champions, boasted six all-Americans: Mark Barron, Dont'a Hightower, Barrett Jones, Dre Kirkpatrick, Trent Richardson, and Courtney

Running back Mark Ingram became Alabama's first Heisman Trophy winner on December 12, 2009. The trophy is awarded annually to the most outstanding college football player. Ingram was later drafted by the New Orleans Saints.

Upshaw. Saban had earned the reputation of being a genius at recruiting top talent. His recruiting team researched candidates meticulously. They looked at everything from a player's weight, height, and flexibility (a linebacker's heels should be touching the ground when he is in his stance, for instance), to his mental strength. This was determined by talking to several friends and family members. Alabama encouraged players to come to the school's summer camp so that coaches could see them in person.

Saban has also been said to push the envelope, and some recruiting rules were seemingly made for him. For instance, Saban was criticized for signing more than twenty-five players. While this was not against the rules at the time, only twenty-five players could be given spots on the roster according to NCAA regulations. The NCAA made a new rule that only twenty-five players could be signed per year.

The Alabama players deserved much of the credit for the team's success. Saban's process required five things of the players: discipline, effort, commitment, toughness, and pride. Exercising those five values, players rose to the expectations of their coach and the Alabama fans. In 2011, they had to rise to a different kind of occasion, when tragedy struck the town of Tuscaloosa.

TRAGEDY, LEGACY & FUTURE

Overnight on April 27 and 28, 2011, a record-breaking 173 tornadoes broke out in the South. Alabama, and Tuscaloosa in particular, were the hardest hit. A tornado as wide as a mile and with winds up to 190 miles (305 kilometers) per hour traveled 6 miles (9.6 km) through the college town.

University of Alabama long snapper Carson Tinker was at home with his girlfriend, Ashley Harrison, when the tornado roared through town. They took cover in a closet, but the house broke apart, and the two were thrown 75 yards (69 meters). Tinker survived the tragedy, but Harrison died from a neck injury. She was one of seven Alabama students who died that day. Their dogs also perished in the storm. When the storm cleared, 50 people had died in Tuscaloosa alone, 240 people statewide, and 297 throughout the South. Doctors reported injuries equivalent to terrible automobile accidents. In Tuscaloosa, seven thousand homes and six hundred businesses were lost. The debris cleared could have filled Bryant-Denny Stadium three times.

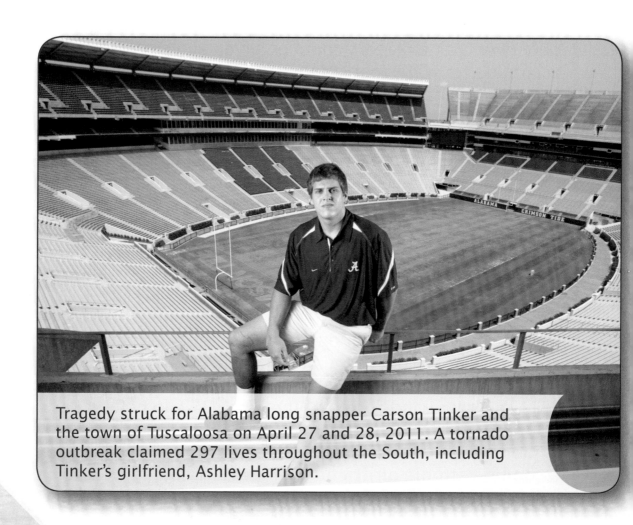

Tragedy struck for Alabama long snapper Carson Tinker and the town of Tuscaloosa on April 27 and 28, 2011. A tornado outbreak claimed 297 lives throughout the South, including Tinker's girlfriend, Ashley Harrison.

Players took to the streets to help their friends and the whole community. Tinker's special teams friends buried his dogs for him. Other teammates helped search for survivors, clear the debris off homes, and raise money for the Red Cross. Help poured in from around the state, including a bus from Auburn carrying football coaches and players. There was a charity flag football game among alumni from Alabama and Auburn. Help came from afar, too. Members of the Louisiana Urban Search and Rescue Team and the Kent State Football Team arrived to help.

Town leaders worked hard to prepare for the season opener in September. They knew that it would help residents take their minds off the terrible storm. The influx of fans would also lift Tuscaloosa's economy. Alabama was playing Kent State, Saban's alma mater. Because Kent State players had helped with the tornado cleanup, word spread among Alabama fans to greet the visitors with cheers, not boos, and that's just what happened.

Two quarterbacks played in the season opener for the Crimson Tide: A. J. McCarron and Phillip Sims. They were both up for the starting quarterback position. Both played well, and Alabama ended up thumping Kent State 48–7. McCarron got the starting spot; Sims later transferred to the University of Virginia to play quarterback. Next, Alabama beat Penn State 27–11. Alabama, ranked number two at the start of the year, went on to win the BCS National Championship game. Seniors had seen forty-eight victories in the course of four years, a record tied with Florida's 2006–2009 seasons.

The team showed no signs of slowing down. In 2012, Alabama was ranked number one in all the polls. They fought off LSU in their closest victory of the season (described in the introduction), though they lost to Texas A&M. Most teams they beat by more than twenty or thirty points. They beat

Georgia in the SEC Championship and Notre Dame in the BCS National Championship game.

There was a shakeup in the NCAA conferences in 2012, with Texas A&M and the University of Missouri joining the SEC. Analysts thought that may mean more recruiting power for SEC teams in Texas and Missouri because games would be shown there on TV. A change was also on the horizon for the system that determines the national champion. Beginning with the 2014 season, there will be a four-team playoff instead of a single BCS game.

Meanwhile, many graduates of the Alabama program have found a welcome home in the NFL. Saban ran an NFL-style offense and defense, which made for a smooth transition between the leagues. Alabama boasted eleven first-round draft picks between 2007 and 2012. In 2012, thirty-nine Alabama alumni were playing in the NFL, along with eleven former players or coaches working as coaches in the NFL.

Legacy is important. Fans are important. Coaches are very important. But every year, a new team takes the field, eleven players at a time, and it is up to them to make it happen. That's how the tide rolls on.

1892: W. G. Little founds the Alabama football team. Alabama plays Auburn University for the first time.

1898: Due to a nationwide controversy over the roughness of the sport, there is no Alabama football team this year.

1907: Alabama earns the name the Crimson Tide.

1915: Denny Field opens, named for school president and football supporter George Denny.

1922: Alabama beats Penn State, a major upset of an eastern powerhouse.

1926: Under coach Wallace Wade, Alabama wins its first national title (for the 1925 season) at the Rose Bowl, defeating the Washington Huskies.

1929: The current stadium opens under the name Denny Stadium. It will undergo many expansions through the years.

1948: The Alabama-Auburn rivalry resumes with an annually scheduled game.

1958: Paul "Bear" Bryant takes on the head coaching position at Alabama.

1970: Alabama loses a historic game against the University of Southern California, which leads to the integration of Alabama and SEC football.

1975: The stadium's name is changed to Bryant-Denny Stadium.

1983: Bryant retires and then dies of heart failure just a few weeks later.

1992: Gene Stallings coaches Alabama in an undefeated season.

2007: Nick Saban becomes head coach of the Crimson Tide.

2009: Alabama is undefeated in the regular season and upsets Florida for the SEC Championship.

2010: Mark Ingram becomes the first Heisman Trophy winner for Alabama.

2011: A tornado devastates Tuscaloosa, killing fifty in the town alone and destroying seven thousand homes; Alabama wins its fourteenth national championship.

2012: Alabama wins its fifteenth national championship.

GLOSSARY

BCS National Championship game The college bowl game that determines the NCAA Division I football champion. "BCS" stands for Bowl Championship Series.

civil rights movement The actions taken, roughly from 1955 to 1968, to achieve equal rights for African Americans.

integration The joining of groups of people who had been segregated.

Iron Bowl The traditional football game played between the University of Alabama and Auburn University.

NCAA National Collegiate Athletic Association; an association representing student athletes that play various sports at participating colleges.

quarterback sack A tackle of the quarterback while he has the ball on or behind the line of scrimmage.

recruiting The act of attracting an athlete to a school by use of scholarships and other means.

Rose Bowl A game held on New Year's Day in Pasadena, California, and the oldest of the bowl games.

running back A player responsible for running the ball.

rushing yards The yards gained by running the ball.

sanction A penalty imposed when a rule is broken.

segregation The separation of people according to skin color or another superficial reason.

Football Canada

100 – 2255, boul. St. Laurent
Ottawa, ON K1G 4K3
Canada
(613) 564-0003
Web site: http://www.footballcanada.com
Football Canada is the governing board of Canadian amateur football, including youth football.

National Collegiate Athletic Association (NCAA)

700 W. Washington Street
P.O. Box 6222
Indianapolis, IN 46206-6222
(317) 917-6222
Web site: http://www.ncaa.org
The NCAA represents student athletes participating in Division I, II, and III sports.

Paul W. Bryant Museum

300 Paul W. Bryant Drive
Tuscaloosa, AL 35487
(866) 772-2327
Web site: http://www.bryantmuseum.com
The Bryant Museum preserves and shares the history of University of Alabama football.

Pop Warner Little Scholars, Inc.

586 Middletown Boulevard, Suite C-100

Langhorne, PA 19047

(215) 752-2691

Web site: http://www.popwarner.com

Pop Warner offers football and cheerleading leagues for ages 5–16.

University of Alabama

Tuscaloosa, AL 35487

(205) 348-6010

Web site: http://www.ua.edu

The University of Alabama is a state university dedicated to learning and research.

USA Football

45 N. Pennsylvania Street, Suite 700

Indianapolis, IN 46204

(877) 5-FOOTBALL (536-6822)

Web site: http://usafootball.com/#headsup

USA Football is the youth development league partner of the NFL and sponsors the Heads Up football safety program.

WEB SITES

Due to the changing nature of Internet links, Rosen Publishing has developed an online list of Web sites related to the subject of this book. This site is updated regularly. Please use this link to access the list:

http://www.rosenlinks.com/AMWT/ALFB

FOR FURTHER READING

Biscup, Agnieszka. *Football: How It Works* (The Science of Sports). Mankato, MN: Capstone, 2010.

Bowling, Lewis. *Alabama Football: More Than a Century of Crimson Tide Glory.* Charleston, SC: The History Press, 2012.

Ford, Tommy. *Tornado to National Title #14: The Story Behind the National Championship Year.* Atlanta, GA: Whitman, 2012.

Frederick, Shane Gerald. *The Best of Everything Football Book.* Mankato, MN: Capstone, 2011.

Green, Tim. *Football Genius.* New York, NY: HarperCollins, 2008.

Holmes, Parker. *The Alabama Crimson Tide.* (Champions of College Football). New York, NY: PowerKids, 2012.

Jacobs, Greg. *The Everything Kids' Football Book* (Everything Kids). Avon, MA: Adams Media, 2008.

Millburg, Steve. *Gone Pro: Alabama: The Crimson Tide Athletes Who Became Legends.* Covington, KT: Clerisy Press, 2012.

Roza, Greg. *Football in the SEC.* New York, NY: Rosen Publishing Group, 2012.

Seidel, Jeff. *Alabama Crimson Tide* (Inside College Football). Minneapolis, MN: ABDO, 2012.

Spinelli, Jerry. *Crash.* New York, NY: Laurel Leaf, 2004.

BIBLIOGRAPHY

Bachman, Rachel, and Ben Cohen. "How Saban Turned the Tide." *Wall Street Journal*, August 28, 2012. Retrieved Oct. 15, 2012 (http://online.wsj.com/article/SB1000087239639044 4914904577617521477347562.html).

Barra, Allen. *The Last Coach: The Life of Paul "Bear" Bryant.* New York, NY: Norton, 2006.

Encyclopedia of Alabama. "Sports and Recreation." Retrieved June 23, 2012 (http://www.encyclopediaofalabama.org/face/ Categories.jsp?path=SportsandRecreation).

ESPN.com. "After Repeated Denials, Saban Takes Bama Job." January 4, 2007. Retrieved October 4, 2012 (http://sports .espn.go.com/ncf/news/story?id=2718488).

ESPN.com. "Alabama Finishes Off Florida for Berth in BCS Title Game." December 5, 2009. Retrieved October 9, 2012 (http://scores.espn.go.com/ncf/recap?gameId=293390333).

Khodabakhshian, Martin, producer. *Roll Tide War Eagle.* ESPN Films 30 for 30. Aired November 8, 2011.

Lewis, Jason. "Black History Month: Desegregating College Football." *Los Angeles Sentinel*, February 9, 2012. Retrieved October 22, 2012 (http://www.lasentinel.net/index .php?option=com_content&view=article&id=979:black -history-month-desegregating-college-football&catid =110&Itemid=200).

Paul W. Bryant Museum. "Timeline." Retrieved June 5, 2012 (http://www.bryantmuseum.com/timeline).

Rolltide.com. Various articles. Retrieved June 2–25, 2012 (http://www.rolltide.com).

Sports Illustrated. "McCarron Has Heisman-like Moment for No. 1 Alabama." SI.com, November 4, 2012. Retrieved November 5, 2012 (http://sportsillustrated .cnn.com/2012/football/ncaa/11/04/alabama-aj -mccarron-heisman-moment-lsu.ap/index.html).

St. John, Warren. *Rammer Jammer Yellow Hammer: A Road Trip into the Heart of Fan Mania.* New York, NY: Crown, 2005.

Tanglao, Leezel. "Tornadoes and Storms Tear Through South; at Least 292 Dead." *ABC World News with Diane Sawyer*, April 28, 2011. Retrieved October 17, 2012 (http:// abcnews.go.com/US/tornadoes-storms-tear-south -292-dead/story?id=13474955#.UJLaGcVfCFg).

University of Alabama. "Bryant-Denny Stadium." Retrieved October 22 2012 (http://tour.ua.edu/tourstops/ bryantdenny.html).

Wade, Don. *Always Alabama.* New York, NY: Touchstone, 2006.

Whiteside, Kelly. "After Tornado, Tuscaloosa Gets Lift from Crimson Tide." *USA Today*, August 30, 2011. Retrieved June 2, 2012 (http://www.usatoday.com/sports/college/ football/sec/story/2011-08-30/After-tornado-Tuscaloosa -gets-lift-from-Crimson-Tide/50197084/1).

INDEX

ABOUT THE AUTHOR

Bridget Heos is the author of more than forty books for children and teens, including *Sports Families: Ronde and Tiki Barber.* She lives in Kansas City with her husband and three sons, whom she cheers on in their football games.

PHOTO CREDITS

Cover, pp. 1, 4 Mike Zarrilli/Getty Images; back cover (goal post) David Lee/Shutterstock.com; pp. 5, 17, 19 © AP Images; p. 8 © Paul W. Bryant Museum, The University of Alabama; p. 9 Robert Abbott Sengstacke/Archive Photos/Getty Images; p. 12 Bob Rosato/Sports Illustrated/Getty Images; p. 13 Manny Millan/Sports Illustrated/Getty Images; p. 22 Heinz Kluetmeier/Sports Illustrated/Getty Images; p. 25 Collegiate Images/Getty Images; p. 27 Jamie Squire/Getty Images; p. 29 Kevin C. Cox/Getty Images; p. 32 Joe Robbins/Getty Images; p. 34 Kelly Kline/Getty Images; p. 36 Simon Bruty/Sports Illustrated/Getty Images; multiple interior page borders and boxed text backgrounds (football) Nickola_Che/Shutterstock.com; pp. 7, 16, 24, 31 from a photo by Jamie Squire/Getty Images; back cover and multiple interior pages background (abstract pattern) © iStockphoto.com/Che McPherson.

Designer: Brian Garvey; Editor: Bethany Bryan; Photo Researcher: Amy Feinberg